G000168692

MEDJUGORJE

by
David Baldwin

*To those who look
to the Sun of Justice,
Jesus Christ*

*All booklets are published thanks to the
generous support of the members of the
Catholic Truth Society*

CATHOLIC TRUTH SOCIETY
PUBLISHERS TO THE HOLY SEE

CONTENTS

With grateful thanks to a Monk of Downside Abbey, my friends - young and not so young - from Youth 2000, and CTS editorial staff.

INTRODUCTION

Medjugorje! To some, this very foreign name may mean nothing; to others, maybe a vague undefined notion of some mysterious happenings in a distant country - probably best avoided. To some others, who may be aware of what is being reported out of Medjugorje, emotions ranging from simple scepticism to active disbelief. To many others, a deep devotion to the Blessed Virgin Mary, prompted by reported appearances over the past years in this little-known Balkan village. It is a name, however, that is gradually gaining prominence in the Catholic consciousness, not only for what it has brought - and continues to bring - but also for the questions, disquiet, and indeed confusion that has come with it.

For it is Medjugorje, an obscure, rural village in the little known country of Bosnia-Herzegovina, that has become over the last twenty years, the site of a widespread international pilgrimage. Despite its geographical isolation away from the main tourist trail, despite its lack of sophistication and modern facilities, despite the ambivalent and sometimes oppressive communist rule of the former Yugoslavia, despite the ragings of the brutal civil wars during the break-up of Yugoslavia, over twenty million people from all corners of the earth have made their way to Medjugorje. Having heard about the reported

apparitions and other happenings they have gone - and continue to go - no doubt with mixed intent: some out of curiosity, some in hope, many seeking, and many to pay homage to Mary, the Mother of God.

Reported apparitions of Our Lady

For it is here that Our Lady - *Gospa* in Croatian - has, since 1981, been reported as regularly 'appearing in apparition' to six local young people. These alleged 'appearances' have given rise to a constant stream of 'messages' which are passed and avidly read round the world, as well as to a declaration of 'ten secrets' to the 'visionaries' which will be revealed to the world within their life time. At the time of writing these happenings continue and have not yet ceased.

All this has given rise to some disquiet within the Church, particularly the local Church. It has given rise to many world-wide charitable movements and organisations radiating from Medjugorje; it has given rise to an outpouring to many of a new spiritual awakening and conversion to God and commitment to His Church. To the Church itself, however, weighing the evidence of the tangible, visible fruits and the reported claims of supernatural elements, it is proving to be a test of caution and prudence in the face of some controversy. This process has been complicated by an unforeseen popular desire that the 'apparitions' be officially recognised and approved by the Church.

The Church's current position, however, is quite clear: "On the basis of investigations so far it cannot be affirmed that one is dealing with supernatural apparitions and revelations" (the Zadar Declaration of 1991). It does, however, leave the matter open to further investigation and assessment - after events at Medjugorje have clearly ceased. This was made clear in a statement from the Congregation for the Doctrine of the Faith in 1998 when, "it would now pertain to the Members of the Episcopal Conference of Bosnia-Herzegovina to possibly take the case again under examination, and, in that case, to issue new declarations". In taking this stance, the Church has to continue treading the delicate path of meeting and serving the needs of those wishing to go to Medjugorje without, in the present circumstances, explicitly authenticating why they go there.

Purpose and contents

Many of the apparitions reported from time to time from all over the world are more often disowned or ignored by the Church - usually for heretical content - at an early stage. But this particular event has been enduring for over twenty one years, and has had a profound effect - and continues to do so - on many people. It is against this rising interest over Medjugorje that an attempt to provide a popular, accurate and balanced account is given by this booklet. It does not presuppose, nor require, any former knowledge of

Medjugorje. Its purpose is to explain the background to, and give a simple, unvarnished account of what is happening in Medjugorje, using authentic sources.

The booklet places Medjugorje geographically and historically; it gives a brief overview as well as a narrative account of the reported events. It describes the place and purpose of apparitions, visions and dreams - and private revelation - within the Church tradition. It explains the Church's current position over Medjugorje, and how this should guide the individual. It displays the fruits coming out of Medjugorje and talks a bit about the so-called visionaries. It summarises the intent of the 'messages' as reported by the visionaries. It gives a personal 'taster' of what the pilgrim may expect 'on the ground' once having arrived there, and tenders the accepted guidance to those who may be contemplating pilgrimage to Medjugorje. The booklet seeks neither to persuade nor dissuade, simply to inform.

Use of terms

In doing so, however, some clarification needs to be made over the use of language when describing the 'events', 'messages', 'apparitions', 'visionaries', 'secrets', 'locutionists', and the like. When referring to these words the reader will also have noticed the deliberate linkage with such terms as 'reported', 'alleged', 'supposed' and 'so-called'. For whilst in 1991 the Church ruled on events taking place at Medjugorje, and has since always adhered to that ruling, it is unlikely to make any further assessment, or any other declaration as to the nature of these happenings until the 'apparitions' are reported as having ceased. But, as the claim of 'supernatural' forms an integral part of these activities they cannot be ignored in the telling of the Medjugorje story.

So, to avoid unnecessary repetition and continuous parenthesising of these qualifying words, which would be ruinous to style and make for fractured reading, the reader is cautioned to bear in mind that these supposed supernatural events are as *reported*, and bear only the subjective value of individual human witness and articulation. There is no intention to contradict or undermine the position that the Church has adopted to date regarding Medjugorje, and this the reader is asked to bear in mind throughout the booklet. This particularly applies in the 'Events' and 'Messages' sections where a simple narrative style has been adopted to depict the reported details of the apparitions, messages and the so-called secrets.

In modern parlance there is a 'health warning' on Medjugorje, over which the Church, having urged caution, reserves the right to re-examine and, if she wishes, to make further declarations.

MEDJUGORJE

As the crow flies Medjugorje lies about 30 kilometres inland from the bright blue Adriatic Sea. The ascent from the Croatian coastal strip is up hair-pin bends and over some rugged hills, crossing into Bosnia-Herzegovina, until reaching a plateau surrounded by hills in the sparsely populated commune area of Citluk. One sees a rocky, harsh country covered by low scrub and maquis; there are few trees. The lower lying plateau bottom has been cleared for cultivation and, whilst not extensive, is fertile and grows tobacco, grape vines, fruit and vegetables. Although of a generally mild Mediterranean climate, the area experiences extremes of weather - with some damp, miserable winter periods, and a drought problem during the burning hot summers.

History

Evidence of human inhabitation goes back to the Early Stone and Bronze Ages. The Romans colonised the area as the province of Dalmatia and from that period onwards, this part of the world, the Balkans, has been a crucible of cruel conflict, subjected to wars, conquest, destruction and occupation, right up until modern times. Although Christianity initially came to the area in the Roman era, the raids of the Barbarian tribes in the 6th and 7th centuries almost completely destroyed the early Church. The Croats who subsequently settled in the region in the late 7th century accepted conversion to Christianity, but as a church described as 'Bosnian' rather than Roman. In the 13th century it was the Franciscans who successfully returned the Church to Rome, and whose presence and influence have remained until this day

However, this peaceful conversion was soon to be totally reversed by the Turkish occupation of 1473. As Christians were not allowed to own land, conversion to Islam was effected relatively easily and swiftly. Those few who hung on to their faith were placed in permanent serfdom. Throughout the Turkish occupation, which ended in 1878, the Franciscan priests alone remained with their flock; the secular clergy, with their bishop, having been driven out to Austria, therein sowing the seeds of some of the tensions that echo round the area today. When relative peace returned to Herzegovina in the 18th century it was the Franciscans who organised a parish system, which included Medjugorje as part of the parish of Brotnjo until 1892, when it was declared a parish in its own right. The secular hierarchy was restored by Pope Leo XIII in 1881, which gradually took over ecclesiastical administration of the whole area.

Church and Cross

The first church for the new parish was completed in 1897, and one can only postulate that it was by some

The parish church of St James at Medjugorje.

extraordinary intervention that led to the church being
dedicated to St James the Greater, the pilgrim Apostle.
Sadly, this first church suffered the effects of earth
tremors and began to crack and subside. The present
church, although started in 1934, was not completed
until 1969, mainly delayed by the ravages of world and
civil war and the prevarication of the subsequent
communist regime. Again, providentially, the size of
this church was designed far in excess of the existing
requirements of that small, rural population.

The village of Medjugorje would be unremarkable,
but for one distinguishing feature - not only physically
striking, but a visible manifestation of a community's
collective devotion to God - the huge concrete cross set
atop a nearby hillside that overlooks the parish. In 1933
the parish priest and parishioners erected this 36 foot
high, 15 ton reinforced concrete cross to "mark the
1900th anniversary of the Passion of Jesus". All the
building materials had to be lugged up this steep, stony
hillside by hand, "old man and boy, youth and girl, they
all competed to do as much as they could to realise this
holy act" notes the parish chronicle. Embedded in the
concrete of the cross is a relic of the True Cross. These
stout efforts, and the resultant cross give, strong
testament to a village's fidelity to the Lord their God.

OVERVIEW

The 24th of June 1981, the feast day of St John the Baptist, will be remembered by the villagers of Medjugorje as a day that was to change their life in some form for the foreseeable future. In the early hours of that morning the village was engulfed in a summer storm of an intensity and ferocity that has not been recalled since. Ground shaking thunder was preceded by continuous, renting lightning strikes, one of which set the post office on fire. The storm departed as swiftly as it arrived. Some hours later, in more tranquil circumstances, six excited local youths reported to their friends and families of having seen on a nearby hillside a beautiful young woman holding a child, who had suddenly and inexplicably appeared before them, beckoning them to approach.

This was the start of a chain of events that was to have continuous local and subsequent, world-wide and Church-wide repercussions. For it was from that day and onwards to the present, that the Blessed Virgin Mary has been supposedly appearing in apparition to those young people, who some twenty one years on, are now well into adulthood. Of the six, described at the time as, "representative of the village, neither good or bad, just like every one else", only three of them were close friends. Whilst these were acquainted with the other

three, they had little else in common, and indeed their
initial coming together to witness and pass on their
extraordinary experience initially frightened and confused
them. The age range between them was also wide, the
four girls of the group were between seventeen and
fifteen, and the two boys were sixteen and ten at the time.

During these apparitions, which have been
experienced collectively and singly, the seers claim that
Our Lady prays and talks to them, as well as having
revealed ten secrets to three of them, whilst the other
three still await the tenth. Messages are also given
specifically for public disclosure. Initially, these were
weekly messages directed specifically to the parishioners
of Medjugorje, but, in January 1987, were redirected to
monthly on the 25th of each month, for promulgation
world-wide, and continue to this day.

Since the beginning, the apparitions continued on a
daily basis to all the children, until December 1982.
Between then and 1998, three of the visionaries had their
apparitions reduced to one a year and on 'special
occasions', as well as having been given the ten secrets,
leaving only three who now experience daily apparitions,
and who await the tenth secret. Added to the initial six
visionaries in 1983 were two ten year old girls who started
having, and still experience, locutions - reportedly hearing
messages from Our Lady. The visionaries experience their
apparitions wherever in the world they may be, as latterly

they have travelled and live abroad. A more detailed and specific account of the visionaries and the locutionists, and the events surrounding them, is given later.

It is a series of events that has far exceeded in time-scale the apparitions approved by the Church, such as Fatima and Lourdes, and to this aspect Medjugorje does not conform. It is a chain of events that survived, and of which news subsequently and inexorably spread - despite the rigours and persecution of communism, despite the scepticism and opposition of the local church hierarchy. It faltered, but blossomed and grew again during and after the bitter civil wars of the break-up of Yugoslavia. It is a chain that has largely, and sometimes quite determinedly, been spread by word of mouth, modern technology, and repute; but, despite its widespread effects and appeal, it appears nonetheless to be a chain triggered by the unsolicited, naïve and transparent belief of those six local young people, a belief to which they have unwaveringly held fast over many years.

Possibly, it is the alleged 'supernatural' nature of these events which, in catching people's imaginations and arousing spiritual awareness, or alternatively inculcating scepticism or disbelief, has caused the principal debate about Medjugorje. But there are also undeniably visible dividends that have emerged, and continue to emerge, from the Medjugorje phenomenon. These 'fruits' - ranging from life changing experiences for countless individuals, to local and world-wide charitable organisations and prayer groups being established - are dynamic and visible. And it is the contrast between the obvious and concrete 'seen', and the mysterious and abstract 'unseen', that lies at the heart of current debate, and over which the Church continues to prayerfully watch.

It is a challenge which demands sympathetic and sober management for the duration of these activities; a management that, on the one hand, would not wish to dismiss out of hand the sincerity of those who believe and hold by these events, and on the other, would not wish to indulge the sentimental, the over-enthusiastic or the wishful thinking, no matter how well meaning. Once the 'apparitions' and related activities have ceased the challenge may be made even more demanding, when the limitations of human cognisance, in further painstaking investigation, aided by prayer and the promptings of the Holy Spirit, may have to re-address the events at Medjugorje and make further declarations if necessary. At present, though, these two elements of seen and unseen may appear mutually exclusive, but whether it be exclusion or inclusion will only become obvious after cessation and investigation. In the meantime, the faithful, the curious, the doubters, may, as those millions before them, be felt drawn to Medjugorje, each in their own way seeking solace, guidance, inspiration or just plain help, and afterwards coming away with their own unique experience of Medjugorje.

APPARITIONS, VISIONS, DREAMS

Apparitions in the Old Testament

Apparitions, visions, dreams - none of these are new to the Christian experience, and indeed they have been known about and experienced by many of the world's religions, from the earliest and most primitive, to the most developed. In the Christian faith they are reported throughout the Old and New Testaments. In the Old Testament Yahweh declares through his prophet Joel, "I shall pour out my Spirit on all humanity. Your sons and daughters shall prophesy, your young people shall see visions, your old people dream dreams" (*Jl* 3:1). Yahweh was in frequent dialogue with His prophets and seers. Abraham was foretold the future of His people in a dream, "Know this for certain, that your descendants will be exiles in a land not their own and be enslaved and oppressed for four hundred years" (*Gn* 15:13). Joseph was promoted from slavery to become the Pharaoh's chancellor by correctly interpreting the Pharaoh's dreams.

Apparitions in the New Testament

In the New Testament angels often appear as frequent messengers of God's will: "In the sixth month the angel Gabriel was sent by God to a town in Galilee called

Nazareth to a virgin betrothed to a man named Joseph" (*Lk* 1:26,27). Joseph was likewise guided by angelic advice, firstly, when he was reassured by an angel to take Mary as his wife, then he was told to flee from Herod to Egypt, and then instructed when it was time to return to Nazareth.

It is through apparitions that the fact of the Resurrection was manifested by Jesus' appearance as the Risen Christ, firstly to Mary Magdalene, and then in other subsequent appearances to the Apostles prior to the Ascension. The most graphic of these apparitions is when he invited Thomas, the doubter, to actually touch and feel His wounds, "Give me your hand; put it into my side" (*Jn* 20:27). The last apparition of Jesus to the Apostles in the Scriptures was of His Ascension, "Now as he blessed them, he withdrew from them and was carried up to heaven" (*ibid v51*). But even after the Ascension, experiences of apparitions continued, as with St Stephen, the first martyr, before he was stoned to death, " 'Look! I can see heaven thrown open,' he said, 'and the Son of Man standing at the right hand of God'." (*Ac* 7:56).

Apparitions in the post-apostolic era

This sort of phenomenon did not, however, cease at the close of the apostolic era - from that time to this day, they have been experienced and reported in much measure and frequency. Early examples are the Christian Anchorites who sought solitude in the desert wastes, and the first monks such as St Anthony of Egypt (251-356), and later, the followers of St Benedict (480-543), all produced visionaries and seers. All the ages have produced the great mystics and visionaries who have so enriched our Church, and ultimately our knowledge of God: St Augustine in the fifth century, St Francis in the twelfth century, St Dominic in the thirteenth, St Philip Neri in the sixteenth, the Curé d'Ars in the nineteenth, St Maximilian Kolbe of the twentieth, to name but a tiny representative sample.

Those apparitions, visions and dreams described in Scripture must unquestionably be received as part of God's Revelation to His people, and accepted, in faith, as they are "written under the inspiration of the Holy Spirit, they have God as their author, and have been handed on as such to the Church herself" (*CCC 105*). In Cardinal Ratzinger's Theological Commentary on the Secrets of Fatima (in *The Message of Fatima*, Congregation for the Doctrine of the Faith, 2000): "It is called 'Revelation' because in it God gradually made himself known to men, to the point of becoming man himself ... " and, in explaining the finality of God's 'public Revelation', "In Christ, God has said everything, that is he has revealed himself completely, and therefore Revelation came to an end with the fulfilment of the mystery of Christ as enunciated in the New Testament".

However, there is a clear link-across from public Revelation - all that revealed in Scripture - to the private revelation of the post-apostolic era, where the *Catechism of the Catholic Church* states, "even if Revelation is already complete, it has not been made fully explicit; it remains for Christian faith gradually to grasp its full significance over the course of the centuries" (*CCC para 66*). This is expanded in the next section, where, "Throughout the ages there have been so-called 'private revelations', some of which have been recognised by the authority of the Church ... Guided by the Magisterium of the Church, the *sensus fidelium* knows how to discern and welcome in these revelations whatever constitutes an authentic call of Christ or his saints to the Church" (*para 67*).

However, before looking at how the Church treats such supernatural events that have occurred after the Scriptures, it will be worth sorting out exactly what is meant by these terms, and as ever, such subjects of technicality and mystery tend to be shrouded by technical and mysterious terminology.

Charismatic Mystical Phenomena

What we are specifically looking at are termed 'Charismatic Mystical Phenomena', of which three possible causes are attributed: God, occult natural power, or diabolical influence. The common name given to these particular mystical phenomena is 'visions', and visions can simply be defined as 'the perception of an object or person that is naturally invisible to mortal beings' (*New Catholic Encyclopedia*). Since the days of St Augustine, mystical writers have generally agreed to separate visions into three categories: corporeal, imaginative and intellectual. We are concerned primarily in this booklet with the corporeal. Critical to understanding this particular phenomenon, is that the object of the vision is seen *physically* by the seer, with the bodily eyes, obeying the normal physical laws of the transmission of light and image. Imaginative and intellectual visions are purely manifestations of the mind and are not seen externally. Those visionaries and mystics, such as St Teresa of Avila, who receive sudden and unmediated illuminations of Divine Truth can be ascribed to having intellectual visions.

Corporeal visions are therefore what can more commonly be termed as apparitions, literally 'appearances', from the Latin *apparitio*, meaning 'attendance'. As described above, they are "a *sensible* manifestation of God, an angel, a saint or any resurrected soul to a living person (or persons) on earth" (*Encyclopedic Dictionary of Religion*). I emphasise the word 'sensible' as taking its literal meaning: 'of the senses' - eyes, ears, nose, touch, even smell. Also within the genre of corporeal visions fall locutions, which are confined solely to the visionary physically hearing the object of the vision, rather than seeing it, and as opposed to 'voices in the head' which is typical of imaginative or intellectual locutions.

"It doesn't seem to me like a revelation from heaven. It is usual in such cases for Our Lord to tell the souls to whom He makes such communications to give their confessor or parish priest an account of what has happened. But this child on the contrary keeps it to herself as far as she can. This may also be a deceit of the devil. We shall see. The future will show us what we are to think about it all". These are the words of the parish priest as reported by Lucia, the surviving Fatima seer, on her first interview with him (*Fatima, in Lucia's Own Words*). They sum up perfectly the Church's initial reaction to any report or claim of supernatural experiences. The Church rightly observes extreme caution and prudence when reacting to such claims - there is a fine line between giving way to the no-doubt good intentions of the devout, or to the clamour of populist devotion spurred on by wishful thinkers, or even worse, to succumbing to some diabolical plot. True discernment of a supernatural and Divine event is a painstaking, prayerful, and often painful process.

Church approval

For example, this is graphically illustrated by the many reported apparitions in the immediate aftermath of Our Lady's appearances at Lourdes - no doubt stimulated by events at Lourdes; of those that were investigated, none were authenticated. Accurate and consistent statistics on apparitions seem hard to come by, but of the many hundreds of reported apparitions from all over the world, only a handful, eighteen by some counts, have been 'accepted' or authenticated by the Church, with one of the earliest being that of Our Lady at Guadalupe in 1531. The most recent acceptance by the Church, as reported in the *Catholic World News* of 29th June 2001, was given in relation to three young African women seers at Kibeho, Rwanda who experienced apparitions of Our Lady on 28th November 1981, and in the course of the following months.

In investigating reported apparitions the Church applies much the same thorough and painstaking process applied for beatification and canonisation. It was Pope Benedict XIV who insisted in his Encyclical *'De Beatificatione et Canonizatione Servorum Dei'* that, "No phenomenon is to be attributed to a supernatural power until all possible natural or diabolical explanation has been investigated and excluded". After being passed on by the parish priest to his bishop as being worthy of further examination, the evaluation process next involves an initial and thorough examination by a formal Commission raised by the diocesan bishop. Commissioners will examine all forms of human trickery and deception, even if well intentioned; they will consider hallucinatory aspects, and thoroughly test the diabolical. The criteria, amongst others, will continually be measured by prudence, natural and medical sciences, and, through theology, the application of intellectual and moral yardsticks. The consensus of credible witnesses will also play a part.

If the bishop is satisfied with the favourable report of his Commission, he will then endorse the event as being supernaturally inspired, that it contains nothing harmful or contrary to faith or morals; and that it is worthy of credibility, reverence and devotion of the faithful. It is important to re-emphasise in the Medjugorje context, that although the Zadar Declaration is the Church's current, definitive position, it is not necessarily the final conclusion, which may only be instigated when it is apparent that the reported apparition activity has ceased.

Once diocesan approval has been given, a lengthy devotional phase should follow, with the faithful demonstrating a life of piety and prayer, self denial and repentance. If the devotion increases and spreads and holds, it can lead to acceptance on behalf of the Church by the Pontiff, and ultimately given formal liturgical recognition such as celebrating the Feast of Our Lady of Fatima (13th May), or the adoption of prayers and devotions such as the Fatima prayer or the Chaplet of Divine Mercy. In doing so the Church emphasises that such approval of private revelations does not further contribute to the 'deposit of the faith' (*CCC 67*), and that the faithful are only required to give the same human belief as they would give to anything else that they hold to be true. If after mature and prayerful reflection a person feels unable to believe an apparition, even though approved by the Church, then they should not feel obliged to maintain assent; however, they should desist from openly dissenting. With so called 'private revelations' the Church's approval never 'enjoins anyone to accept them with the certitude of divine faith'.

Of the few accepted apparitions it is striking that the majority and most popular feature Mary. Donal Foley, in his CTS booklet *Apparitions of Mary* relates Mary's appearances as preordained responses to major secular events in history, such as Guadalupe to the Reformation, Lourdes to the Enlightenment, Fatima to the fall of communism and nazism. In Foley's words, "As the spiritual Mother of mankind she cannot stand idly by and watch humanity destroy itself through sin and selfishness. Her apparitions have played a large part in the major Catholic renewals of recent centuries."

There is no doubt that Mary strikes a very deep and resonant chord with the Faithful: she who is totally obedient; she who unhesitatingly made the first conscious act of Christian faith; she who experienced the supreme joy of the birth of her Son and suffered the ultimate agony and despair of His death; she who was granted the highest privilege of being the Ark of the New Covenant, and the greatest recognition of being crowned Queen of Heaven and earth. "We believe that the Holy Mother of God, the new Eve, Mother of the Church, continues in heaven to exercise her maternal role on behalf of the members of Christ" (*CCC 975*).

THE CHURCH'S POSITION

The Zadar Declaration

"The Bishops, from the very beginning, have been following the events of Medjugorje through the bishop of the Diocese (Mostar), the Bishop's Commission and the Commission of the Bishops' Conference of Yugoslavia on Medjugorje.

On the basis of the investigations so far it cannot be affirmed that one is dealing with supernatural apparitions and revelations.

However, the numerous gatherings of the faithful from different parts of the world, who come to Medjugorje, prompted both by motives of belief and various other motives, require the attention and pastoral care in the first place of the diocesan bishop and with him of the other bishops also, so that in Medjugorje and everything connected with it, a healthy devotion to the Blessed Virgin Mary may be promoted in accordance with the teaching of the Church.

For this purpose the bishops will issue specially suitable liturgical-pastoral directives. Likewise, through their Commission they will continue to keep up with and investigate the entire event in Medjugorje."

Thus goes the crucial statement - known as the Zadar Declaration - issued unanimously by the Bishop's

Conference of former Yugoslavia in April 1991 in response to a growing need for clarification over Medjugorje. Its brevity contrasts not only with the various activities at Medjugorje over those first ten years, but also the deliberations of the diocesan bishop (Mostar) and the investigations of the Bishop's Commissions that sat during that period. It is crucial because it is the official pronouncement of the Church's view over Medjugorje at that time, and remains crucial, because it continues to be the Church's view, to which enquirers, from whatever level, are inevitably referred.

Key components

There are two key components to the Declaration which may be worth examining in the interests of maintaining balance and understanding. The first is, "it cannot be affirmed that one is dealing with supernatural apparitions and revelations". In looking at this statement one needs to study the subtle difference in the terminology used by the Church when categorising supernatural events. Regarding Medjugorje, the key phrase 'it cannot be affirmed that one is dealing with supernatural events' translates into Latin as, *'non constat de supernaturalitate'*. The other phrase which could have been deployed is, *'constat de non supernaturalitate'* which translates as, 'it is affirmed that there are no supernatural occurrences'. The negative in the former statement (*non constat*) is only against current affirmation, whilst the negative in the latter category (*constat de non*) is laid against supernatural happenings. Some would argue that *'non constat'*, as stated in Zadar, leaves the matter open to further assessment whilst *'constat de non'* clearly would have closed down any further discussion of any supposed supernatural manifestations.

In seeking support for such interpretation some would look to the letter written in May 1998 by Archbishop Tarcisio Bertone, Secretary to the Congregation for the Doctrine of the Faith (CDF), to Msgr Gilbert Aubry Bishop of St Denis (Reunion Island) to clarify this specific issue. Archbishop Bertone commented, "Since the division of Yugoslavia into different independent nations, it would now pertain to the members of the Episcopal Conference of Bosnia-Herzegovina to perhaps reopen the examination of this case, and to make any new pronouncements that might be called for". This may well leave room for further investigations of whatever scope and persuasion, but only when it is apparent that these events have ceased. As this key letter from CDF also addresses other Medjugorje issues, the full text is given at the Appendix.

The second component of the Declaration is the acknowledgement by the Church of the "numerous gatherings of the faithful from different parts of the world" and their need for "attention and pastoral care" whilst ensuring that "a healthy devotion to the Blessed Virgin Mary may be promoted in accordance with the teaching of the Church". It would seem that this does not deny the faithful their wishes to make private pilgrimage to Medjugorje, and indeed exhorts the diocesan and other bishops to ensure that they provide the correct level and content of pastoral support for the pilgrims.

Immediately succeeding the Zadar Declaration a newly formed liturgical and pastoral Commission, to include the pastoral staff of the parish of Medjugorje, was set up, and was to have met on 27th June 1991. This was unfortunately forestalled by the outbreak of civil war in Yugoslavia on the 25th of June, the tenth anniversary of the start of the apparitions being reported.

Lead up to Zadar

The road to Zadar, and beyond, was, and still is, not easy. For when looking at the events at Medjugorje one cannot ignore the at times painful and confusing human incongruity that has been generated, and without getting too entangled in the details of this conflicting and emotional debate a very brief flavour follows.

When the apparitions were first reported, the bishop at Mostar, Bishop Pavao Zanic, was reported as taking a great deal of interest in them, visiting the parish and talking to the 'visionaries' and priests, and going on record as believing the young people's claims. Yet, within a short period of having voiced this support, he was seen to change his view. Some accounts of this reversal recall the inherent and ongoing diocesan tensions as the new Bishop started to put in place plans for reorganising the parishes within his diocese (the so-called 'Herzegovina question'). For in 1980, before the reports of apparitions, the newly enthroned Bishop of Mostar was in the process of reorganising his parishes by replacing some of the Franciscan priests with diocesan priests - to the dismay of parishioners and Franciscans. Although Medjugorje was not directly involved in this reorganisation, the Franciscan presence there, and the subsequent events at Medjugorje, inevitably became entangled in what may normally have been a short-lived and prosaic affair of parish politics.

Other accounts as to the bishop's change of mind treat of reported messages via the 'visionaries' from Our Lady disagreeing with the bishop's stance, and lending strong support to the Franciscans. Whatever the facts, one may also have to add the nature of the national volatility, and these matters, which could have been discreetly kept within the diocese, were escalated to emotional and public heights.

It should be emphasised that none of the foregoing is intended to undermine the Bishop of Mostar's right to his view as the Ordinary of the place. The episode should also be seen within the wider contemporary and secular context of the stifling communist regime in place at the time, the delicate political situation prevailing in Europe during the collapse of the Eastern bloc, and latterly, the chaos and conflict of civil war that raged throughout the region, all of which must have had such devastating effects on everybody's lives, and could not have been conducive to calm and clear discernment from any side.

Bishop's Commissions

During the ten years leading up to the Zadar Declaration there were public, lengthy and at times heated debate over what was, or was not, going on at Medjugorje. A Commission of four members was set up by the Bishop of Mostar in January 1982 to examine the events in the parish of Medjugorje, with, unusually, himself as the leading member; it was enlarged at the beginning of 1984 to twenty people. The interim conclusions were that there was insufficient scientific documentation in support of reported healings, and that it disapproved of any organised pilgrimage to Medjugorje.

These conclusions were supported by the Episcopal Conference of Yugoslavia in October 1984. A lengthy statement made at the time by the Bishop of Mostar ended with, "all this emotional excitement over Medjugorje is destined, sooner or later, to fizzle out into nothing, like a balloon bursting or like soap bubbles, and then there will be great disappointment and disgrace for the authority of the Church, who, with some of its responsible people, have favoured hope and have considered the apparitions authentic without waiting for the official judgement".

In maintaining not only this line, but in going further, the Bishop of Mostar, has also stated that, "My conviction and my position is not only *non constat de supernaturalitate,* but *constat de non supernaturalitate* of apparitions and revelations in Medjugorje" (letter to French weekly *'Famille Chretienne'*). This view was shared by his successor Msgr Ratko Peric, when he declared, "Neither the diocesan bishop ... or any other competent person, have until now declared the parish church of St James as a Marian shrine, nor confirmed the cult of Our Lady based on the supposed apparitions ... Anyone acting in an opposite manner, is acting expressly against the official position of the Church, which after 14 years of supposed apparitions and developed commercial propaganda, are still valid in the Church." (*Prijestolje Mudrosti,* Mostar, 1995).

Underlying tensions

However, other views also emerged over the period, such as that of Archbishop Franic of neighbouring Split, who made a statement to the Yugoslav Episcopal Conference in April 1985, saying, amongst other supportive remarks, "Medjugorje gives great and manifest fruits of prayer, of fasting and of conversion. The devil could not have produced such fruits in four years; it would have destroyed his kingdom ... For my own part, I hold that, allowing for human factors, these events are of themselves supernatural". In a further lengthy statement Franic elaborated in September

1987 with, "... all we who go to Medjugorje must go with the firm decision that we shall be obedient to the final judgement of the Church. Up to that point we may have our own 'opinion' about these events, but not 'belief' in those events. Therefore it is not proper to speak about the messages of Medjugorje from the altar, nor is it proper to attack these events in the name of God and of the Church as mendacious and diabolical" (as quoted in the *Tablet*, October 1987).

Another senior cleric in the region, Cardinal Franjo Kuharic, Archbishop of Zagreb, went on record in August 1993, with a more assuaging, but nonetheless contradictory and potentially confusing approach, saying: "After three years of studies by the Commission, we, the bishops, have accepted Medjugorje as a Shrine, as a sanctuary. This means that we have nothing against the veneration of the Mother of God in accordance with the teaching of the Church and our faith... This is why we leave this question to further studies of the Church. The Church is not in haste".

Meanwhile, in Medjugorje, the Franciscan friars have continued about their pastoral business with their powerful and eloquent preaching. They do this with a doggedness and fidelity rooted in their centuries' long service to their parishioners, which since in recent times has survived savage persecution by the communist regime, disbelief from a world at large, and scepticism from their own church hierarchy. In their eyes they are discharging the duty laid on them by Zadar of providing the pastoral care called for, which they do daily with a small army of interpreters, talking to that large army of transient pilgrims.

Despite these underlying tensions, it is apparent that great efforts continue to be made by all sides to maintain a consistent approach, an approach which bears in mind principally the pastoral care of the many hundreds of thousands of pilgrims. One hopes that the great majority come in good faith, simply seeking spiritual succour, not human confusion. For example, on 14th June 2001 it was reported that the Bishop of Mostar confirmed 72 candidates in the parish church of St James, and whilst his homily included his stated belief against the supernatural character of the apparitions, he nonetheless emphasised his satisfaction at the way in which the parish was being administered. He also emphasised the importance of the unity of the Catholic church. In a lovely human touch that sought to reassure, this particular communiqué from Medjugorje ended with, "After the solemn Eucharistic celebration, Msgr Ratko Peric remained in friendly conversation with priests in the Presbytery". The official Medjugorje website also posts, in an outward act of obedience and of continuing reassurance, the statement, "All Franciscan Friars serving in the parish of St James in Medjugorje are here with the permission of the local Bishop, Msgr Ratko Peric, and all possess their canonical jurisdiction for exercising their priestly ministry".

Perspectives

The latest Church teaching over private revelations was
issued by the Congregation for the Doctrine of the Faith
in its 2000 document *'The Message of Fatima'*. In his
theological commentary Cardinal Joseph Ratzinger
quotes Saint Paul in his First Letter to the Thessalonians,
"Do not quench the Spirit, do not despise prophesying,
but test everything, holding fast to what is good" (5:19-
21). In developing this theme, Cardinal Ratzinger goes
on, "In every age the Church has received the charism of
prophesy, which must be scrutinised but not scorned". In
linking the prophetic word as, "warning or a consolation,
or both together" with how to interpret "the signs of the
times" he says, "To interpret the signs of the times in the
light of faith means to recognise the presence of Christ in
every age. In the private revelations approved by the
Church - and therefore also in Fatima - this is the point:
they help us to understand the signs of the times and to
respond to them rightly in faith."

   In dealing specifically with the criterion for the truth and
value of private revelation he states that it is, "orientation
to Christ himself. When it leads us away from him, when it
becomes independent of him or even presents itself as
another and better plan of salvation, more important than
the Gospel, then it certainly does not come from the Holy
Spirit, who guides us more deeply into the Gospel, not
away from it". These thoughts are profound, but they are

also accessible and understandable by any reasonably well instructed and informed person - they are straightforward enough to be objectively applied and tested by anyone studying, going, or having been, to Medjugorje.

Ratzinger continues, "But in all this there must be a nurturing of faith, hope and love, which are the unchanging path to salvation for everyone. We might add that private revelations often spring from popular piety and leave their stamp on it, giving it a new impulse and opening the way for new forms of it ... Popular piety is a sign that the faith is spreading its roots into the hearts of the people in such a way that it reaches into daily life".

Having looked at current teaching it may now be helpful to give, by way of further background, a longer perspective to the Church's position regarding private revelations. For example Pope Urban VIII (1623-44) made a significant statement over reported supernatural events, "In cases like this (apparitions), it is better to believe than not to believe, for, if you believe, and it is proven true, you will be happy that you have believed, because our Holy Mother asked it. If you believe, and it should be proven false, you will receive all the blessings as if it had been true, because you believed it to be true". This was followed, in the same century, with the words of the classic definition by Cardinal Prospero Lambertini, the future Pope Benedict XIV (1675-1758): "An assent of Catholic faith is not due to revelations approved in this way ... (but) rather an assent of human faith in keeping with the requirements of prudence, which puts them before us as probable and credible to piety".

In contemporary terms we read from the Vatican II Document, *Lumen Gentium* 12: "Whether these charisms be very remarkable or more simple and widely diffused, they are to be received with thanksgiving and consolation since they are fitting and useful for the needs of the Church. Extraordinary gifts are not to be rashly desired, nor is it from them that the fruits of apostolic labours are to be presumptuously expected. Those who have charge over the Church should judge their genuineness and proper use of these gifts through their office, not indeed to extinguish the spirit, but to test all things and hold fast to what is good (cf. 1 *Th* 5:12 & 19-21)".

Lambertini's quote given above was used by Cardinal Ratzinger in his Theological Commentary; he also quotes the Flemish theologian E. Dhanis, who identifies three clear components for the ecclesiastical approval of private revelations: the message contains nothing contrary to faith or morals; it is lawful to make it public; and the faithful are authorised to accept it with prudence. There is no reason to doubt that Dhanis' criteria would be strictly applied whenever the case for Medjugorje is further examined.

But this further examination and any further declarations by the Church on the authenticity of the reported apparitions of Our Lady at Medjugorje would most likely only be made on cessation of these events and any direct and associated activity which may involve the so called secrets. As stated earlier, the Vatican has clearly made this, "the concern of the Bishops' Conference of Bosnia and Herzegovina to eventually re-examine this case and to publish new declarations". The Chairman of the Commission tasked by Rome to investigate Medjugorje is currently Bishop Dr Franjo Komarica of Banja Luka. When asked in a recent interview (February 2002) how he personally perceived the phenomenon at Medjugorje, he replied (in part) "... the future will show how the phenomenon at Medjugorje will develop, within itself, and within the Church as a whole. In the end one fact will remain, as the late Bishop Franic said at the beginning, when he tried to protect the visionaries against the fierce attacks from the then powerful regime. He quoted Gamaliel: "If it comes from God it will last, if it is man made, it will simply cease to exist".

EVENTS: 1981 - 2002

The beginnings

"Then we too saw her. Ivan fled straightaway, climbing over a fence. He left the apples and everything he had ... I remained and I looked. It was the outline of a marvellous young girl. She held a child in her arms. She was looking after him. She would cover him and then show him to us. Several times she beckoned to us with her hand ... we were too frightened to come near her ...". There are many accounts and versions as to how the supposed apparitions at Medjugorje started. This is the exact narrative - given in Michael O'Carroll's book *'Medjugorje - Facts, Documents, Theology'* - of Vicka Ivankovic, an intelligent, articulate member of the visionary group given in December 1983 of the events that she experienced in the early evening of 24th June 1981, on a hillside near Medjugorje. Five other young people were with her for this first apparition, after which they all returned to their homes where, "we told everything", and, "some believed. Others were astonished".

On the second day, 25th June, four of the original group, joined by two others, went to the same spot because, "If it was really Our Lady perhaps she would come back ... Suddenly the light shone out, Our Lady was there ... this time there was no child ...". After they had raced up the

most inaccessible terrain of rocks and brambles without any
ill effect, she reported that they prayed with Our Lady, and
she was described as, "Wonderful! Smiling, gay ... there are
no words to describe her".

The visionaries

Who, then, are these young people, who for whatever
purpose, find themselves undergoing this experience?
The eldest, 17 at the time, is Vicka (pronounced
'Vitska') Ivankovic; she is extrovert, quick witted,
intelligent and forthright.

Next, at 16, is Mirjana Dragicevic, who at the time was
spending the summer holidays with her grandmother; she is
noted as "a very private person - yet gracious and possessing
a measure of intellectual poise ... her anguish at the perilous
state of the world is evident ... so is her compassion for those
who don't know God". Marija Pavlovic, daughter of a
farmer, is in a family of six. She is described as "sensitive
and thoughtful", "a natural leader ... with a gentle, quiet,
loving spirit, and her inner joy is evident in the sparkle in her
eye". Next there is Ivan Dragicevic (no relation to Mirjana),
16, a gentle, pensive boy, "self contained and intense".

Ivanka Ivankovic was 15, her mother had died in May
of 1981. She is unassuming and uncomplicated, "quiet
and hardworking, shy yet sensitive ... with an underlying
tranquillity - and a gentle sense of humour occasionally
bubbles up". Jakov Colo is the youngest, being ten at the

time. Abandoned by his father when he was eight, he then suffered the death of his mother at twelve, but in Jan Connell's book *'Interviews with the Visionaries'*, from where most of the above descriptions come, his youthful demeanour and nonchalance is belied by the depth in his eyes: "Here was a young man who seemed at home in the presence of God".

The early days

On the third day the excited but apprehensive children were waiting, when a presence higher up the hill was indicated with three distinctive flashes of light, also reportedly seen by the many others present. Vicka, on the advice of older villagers, had taken and sprinkled holy water at the apparition where, "I said in a loud voice: 'If you are Our Lady, stay with us; if you are not, leave us'. She smiled, I think she was pleased". On this day, significantly, one of the seers, Mirjana, asked her name and she replied, "I am the Blessed Virgin Mary".

The appearances continued on the fourth, fifth and sixth days, prompting the parish priest, Father Jozo Zovko, to start quizzing the children in earnest. Inevitably, news of the apparitions had spread, and large crowds were now starting to gather at the scene. For a marxist regime such large gatherings with Christian intent were not popular. On the morning of the sixth day the children and relatives were required by the authorities to go to the nearby town

of Mostar, by ambulance, for 'psychiatric investigations'.
There they were intimidated and mocked, including being
taken for a visit to the morgue.

On their return later that day, the appearances happened
as before - and it was also the start of the many reported
incidents emanating from them. The first healing was
reported - a child close to death recommended to Our Lady
by one of the visionaries was healed.

Over the ensuing days the authorities maintained pressure
on the young visionaries by harassing them and their parents
in various ways. The apparitions continued in various
locations, including now the church presbytery. After initial,
quite understandable scepticism, the parish priest, Father Jozo,
became the visionaries' strongest champion. On one occasion
when he was in the church and the police were searching for
the visionaries, he tells of distinctly hearing a voice saying,
"Come out and protect the children". His staunch and active
testimony made him the scapegoat for the 'unrest' at
Medjugorje, and earned him a three and a half year prison
sentence for causing sedition. The sentence was commuted to
eighteen months as a result of protests from abroad.

As the apparitions reportedly continued on into
September 1981, there was speculation as to how long
they would go on. At Lourdes, Our Lady had appeared 18
times to Bernadette over six months, and it was assumed
that Medjugorje would experience a similar number of
appearances, but they continued on into 1982.

Changes

The first sign of any change to this routine came in December 1982, when Mirjana reported that Christmas Day would be the last of her daily apparitions. This change heralded the start of a new pattern in the cycle of apparitions, and a subsequent revealing of the roles that each visionary would fulfil. For ease of digestibility the visionaries' current involvement is summarised:

• Mirjana ceased daily apparitions on 25th December 1982. She currently receives apparitions on the 2nd of each month, with an annual apparition on her birthday (18th March). She has received the ten secrets, and her special mission is to pray for unbelievers. Mirjana has also been nominated as the visionary who will reveal, through a nominated priest, the ten secrets.

• Ivanka stopped having daily apparitions in May 1985. She has an annual apparition on the anniversary of the appearances (24th June), has received the ten secrets, and her special mission is to pray for families.

• Jakov saw his last daily apparition in 1998, as well as receiving the tenth secret. His annual apparition is Christmas Day, and his special mission is to pray for the sick and the handicapped.

• Marija continues to receive daily apparitions, has received nine of the secrets, and her special role is to pray for the souls in Purgatory and nuns. She has also been selected to receive and pass on to the world Our Lady's monthly message on the 25th of each month.

• Vicka receives daily apparitions and has been given nine of the secrets; her mission is to pray for the sick and the handicapped.

• Ivan continues to receive daily apparitions, has received nine of the secrets, and his special mission is to pray for youth and for priests.

Locutions

With the apparitions continuing on into 1983, a new dimension was added to the happenings at Medjugorje. A few days after Mirjana had received her last daily apparition, Jelena Vasilij, a ten year old local girl, started to receive locutions, identifying the speaker as Our Lady. Three months later, another ten year old, Marijana Vasilij, a close friend but not a relative, also claimed to have received the same charism of locution. Although complementary to the mission of the visionaries, the emphasis to the locutionists appears to be more on spirituality and the need for prayer through established prayer groups.

The messages regularly received

March 1984 saw another change in the pattern of apparitions and messages. Weekly messages were now reported as being given direct to, and for, the parish every Thursday evening, through Marija. After the initial enthusiasm of the parishioners, church attendance dwindled again some weeks later. It was only after a direct admonition through the message, "Even though I had a special message for the parish to awake the faith of every believer, I do not wish to force anyone to anything he doesn't feel or doesn't want", that attendance rose again, and has been sustained. Many visiting pilgrims have been inspired by the community's fidelity since that time.

The 25th March 1984 saw the passing of the thousandth day of continuous apparitions at Medjugorje, with the message, "Rejoice with me and with my angels, because a part of my plan has already been realised. Many have been converted, but many do not want to be converted. Pray!".

In the continuing development of the delivery of the messages, the announcement came in January 1987 that the weekly Thursday message was to be reduced to once a month. In response to speculation that this was a sign of a wind-down and eventual termination of the apparitions, the visionaries assured the pilgrims that this change was simply an extension of grace. It was also made clear that the messages were destined for wide publication. To this day the messages of the 25th of every month are received

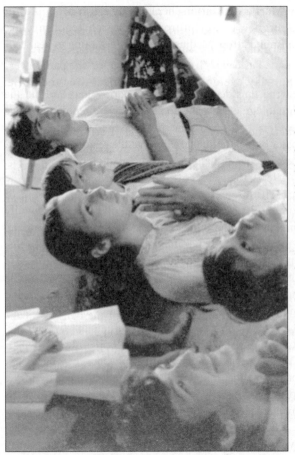

Vicka, Jakov, Ivanka, Marija and Ivan during an 'apparition' in the chapel.

by Marija, and after checking by certain people for adherence to Scripture and Church teaching, are transmitted from Medjugorje to those waiting to hear.

War

Having thus described the visionaries, and laid out the chronology of how the apparitions were reported to have developed, it is now time to weave in to this framework a major burden of human folly that the region had to suffer: the particular brutalities and cruelty of civil war.

1986, the year of the 5th anniversary of the apparitions, heralded the start of the crumbling of communist regimes, starting in Poland, and gradually spreading to the other countries in and around Europe. Yugoslavia, a disparate mix of ethnicity and faiths, hitherto held together by the grim application of a totalitarian police state, also began to come apart, as the individual strands started to try and break away and find and express their own separate identities and aspirations.

Croatia, following the successful attempt by Slovenia some months before, declared itself independent of Yugoslavia on 25th June 1991, - coincidence or otherwise, many note that this was also the tenth anniversary of the apparitions. Within a very short space of time Croatia was involved in an all out struggle for survival.

On 6th April 92 the inevitable happened. War spilled over into Bosnia-Herzegovina with an invasion by insurgent Bosnian Serbs supported by the Yugoslavian army. The war raged in the area round Medjugorje. The town of Mostar, 17 miles from Medjugorje, suffered severe war damage; bombs fell on Citluk only three miles away. In early May, Medjugorje itself was bombed, but it was ineffectual, the bombs either falling high above the village or not detonating.

During this painful period of civil war, pilgrimage to Medjugorje slowed right down. Many at the time felt that the forces of evil may have achieved the aim of suffocating the pilgrim spirit. The March 1992 message was pessimistic: "Satan is playing with you and with your souls, and I cannot help you because you are far from my heart". But there was also a note of reassurance, "Know, dear children, that when something is good, you have to persevere in the good and not think, 'God does not see me, He is not listening, He is not helping'... Therefore, pray, live my message and then you will see the miracle of God's love in your everyday life".

Response to war

Despite the death and destruction, this dark and brutal war appeared to bring forth more abundant fruit from Medjugorje. For the international response against the war was provision of cash, medicines, supplies and physical assistance, as well as a concerted prayer effort from the many world wide associations and prayer groups. Medjugorje in effect became a physical focus point for international relief and charitable effort in the region; one commentator reported, "in spite of the war, the grace of Medjugorje was continuing". Gradually, there was also an increase in pilgrim numbers, and the twelfth anniversary in 1993 saw a crowd of nearly 30,000 pilgrims gathering to celebrate.

In 1994, although fighting continued fiercely in localised areas, particularly Mostar, there were signs that the war was winding down. Medjugorje by now was a major refugee centre and channel of aid, largely brought in initially by pilgrims in their suitcases - hence known as the 'suitcase brigade' - from all over the world. Major relief activity continued into 1995. Organisations such as Caritas, founded in Birmingham, Alabama, were sources of many millions of dollars of donations and other aid. Other, similar relief programmes were underway from many other countries round the world, including technicians, doctors, nurses and teachers who went to the area.

By 1998 the long prayed and hoped for cessation of major fighting in the area came about. As on many other occasions, peace was the theme of the October 1998 message; "Today I call you to open yourselves completely to me so that I may transform you and lead you to the heart of my Son, Jesus, so that He can fill you with His love. Only in this way, little children, will you find true peace, the peace that only God gives you."

Tests on the visionaries

As the apparitions continue, so do the lives of the visionaries. From the very early days they have been the subject of curiosity to the scientific world, mainly being tested through medical and psychological procedures, some of them intrusive and lacking in dignity. These have varied from the rather crude, early attempts by the communist authorities to discredit the visionaries, to the rigorous, sophisticated and structured investigations of specialists in the field of neurology and neuro-psychiatry and other related specialist areas, many of whom were drawn independently to Medjugorje.

A Doctor Magatti studied the reaction of the visionaries to stimuli in moments of ecstasy, and concluded that their state was genuine and their neurological condition one of absolute normality.

A Professor Henry Joyeux who went to Medjugorje in pursuit of his interest in "all phenomena which science finds inexplicable" took encephalograms during the ecstasy, and concluded that there were no signs of hallucination, epileptic manifestation, hysteria or dream state. A Doctor Frigerio applied an electronic instrument to the eyes, ears and mouths of the visionaries during the ecstasy and discovered that they had no cornea reaction; this, he submitted, ruled out play acting, in which they would be unable to repress cornea reaction. He also demonstrated that their eyes did not see objects put before them while the ecstasy lasts.

Some of the scientists were non-believers, and one, Doctor Marco Margnelli, a specialist in ecstasy and altered states of consciousness, went to Medjugorje, "ready to welcome any evidence that would contradict it or show up a fake". After his investigations he concluded, "If anyone had told me these things before my journey here, I would have laughed at it. We are certainly in the presence of an extremely interesting phenomenon. Whether we are dealing with an authentic apparition or something else that we cannot explain, I cannot say; it is a question I prefer not to put to myself". Doctor Margnelli is now a practising Catholic.

One of the latest studies is by Doctor James Pandarakalam, and published in the *Journal of Scientific Exploration* in the summer of 2001. It gives a wide summary of the investigations made on the seers, and concludes *inter alia,* "The medical observations and synchronisms suggests that the Medjugorje visionaries are responding to an outside power and not internal stimuli. The dual modes of perception also suggest that there is a non-physical agent in front of the visionaries. The stronger motivation on the part of the apparition compared with the percipients, collective percipience and quasi-physical features of the apparition, and the limitless loving capacity of the apparition, point towards a true apparitional occurrence at Medjugorje".

The Visionaries today

Despite their experiences, which includes the added pressures of intense public scrutiny, the visionaries appear to have followed the expected patterns of teenagers moving into adult maturity. Ivanka married her childhood friend in June 1986, they have two sons and a daughter, and continue to live near Medjugorje. Mirjana married her childhood friend Marko Soldo in September 1989, and have two daughters; they live in Medjugorje. Jakov married an Italian girl in 1993, they have a son and a daughter and live in Medjugorje. Marija also married in 1993, and subsequently went to live in Italy, from where she continues to receive the monthly messages. She has three sons. Ivan's life was interrupted by a period of military conscription, and in October 1994 he married an American. Vicka, who continues to impart the Medjugorje message to visiting pilgrims, was married in January 2002. In a recent interview she pledged that she would be, "at my post (the stairs of the blue house) most mornings! I will not have to change my mission, I know where I belong".

MEDJUGORJE MESSAGE

Much mention has been made in the preceding pages of the messages being given to the visionaries. Now we will examine the themes of these messages - the so called 'unseen fruits' of Medjugorje.

Firstly, it should be emphasised that in reported 'apparitions' it is generally the Church's practice to rebut anything purportedly coming from a divine source if it contains any suggestion of heresy or impropriety against the Church's teaching. Many hundreds of messages have come out of Medjugorje over a long period of time. While no detailed official examination or declaration on these messages has yet been made by the Church since the Zadar Declaration in 1991, they all have been subject to critical scrutiny by the priests at Medjugorje, and Medjugorje watchers round the world.

The criteria, which any adequately instructed Catholic could apply, even if as crudely as 'a finger to the wind', is that stated in para 67 of *The Catechism of the Catholic Church,* that the role of private revelation is not to "improve or complete Christ's definitive Revelation, but to help live more fully by it in a certain period of history", and, "Christian faith cannot accept 'revelations' that claim to surpass or correct the Revelation of which Christ is the fulfilment ...".

Cardinal Ratzinger underpins this further in his Theological Commentary, "The criterion for the truth and value of a private revelation is therefore its orientation to Christ himself. When it leads us away from him, when it becomes independent of him or even presents itself as another and better plan of salvation, then it certainly does not come from the Holy Spirit, who guides us more deeply into the Gospel and not away from it" (*The Message of Fatima*, Congregation of the Doctrine of the Faith, 2000).

What then is at the heart of these messages? In the first place, one may apply the criteria of the *Catechism* para 67 and that of Cardinal Ratzinger already mentioned, to test whether the messages to date are simple, totally God centred and solidly orthodox. It should be noted that there is an emphasis that what is being said is urgent, and the faithful should heed this sense of urgency. The core message is a call to conversion, a conversion back to God. To many Catholics this word may seem puzzling - after all are we not 'converted' at baptism? To obtain the true and full meaning of this word we need to turn to the *Catechism*, which describes Conversion as, "interior repentance" which is "a radical reorientation of our whole life, a return, a conversion to God with all our heart, an end of sin, a turning away from evil, with repugnance towards the evil actions we have committed" (*CCC 1431*). How many of us actually know this and attempt to actively focus on this conversion effort? Know it or not, it is a constant call coming out of the Medjugorje messages. Put succinctly by St Ambrose, "There are water and tears: the water of baptism and the tears of repentance".

Five 'weapons of salvation'

To deliver and maintain this Conversion the messages describe, 'five weapons of salvation' by calling us all to pray, fast, read the Scriptures, confess, and receive the Eucharist at Mass. Simple, orthodox, yet demanding.

Prayer is very much at the centre of this cry for Conversion, and is the most frequent theme coming out of Medjugorje, "Without unceasing prayer, you cannot experience the beauty and greatness of the grace which God is offering you". In regard to prayer we are also implored to pray with the heart, "Today I invite you to pray with your heart and not only through habit".

On the subject of fasting, we are invited to fast, "on bread and water. Through fasting and prayer one can stop wars, one can suspend the natural laws of nature ... Everyone except the sick has to fast". Of course fasting is not a new discipline, and there are many examples of fasting throughout the Bible. Jesus fasted frequently, and asserted that certain devils "can be cast out in no other way except by prayer and fasting" (*Mk 9:29*). We are also referred to other forms of reduction in self-centred indulgences, such as smoking, drinking, watching television.

There is insistence on daily reading of the Bible. "Dear children, today I call you to read the Bible every day in your homes, and let it be in a visible place so as always to encourage you to read it and pray".

We are asked for monthly confession, with a clear explanation that it should not turn into a monthly habitual ritual, "Confession should give impulse to your faith. It should stimulate you and bring you closer to Jesus. If confession does not mean anything for you, really, you will be converted with real difficulty".

"Let the Holy Mass be your life", is the unequivocal message regarding the fifth weapon of salvation, the Holy Eucharist. Vicka tells us that Our Lady sees the Mass as "the most important and most holy moment in our lives. We have to be prepared and pure to receive Jesus with a great respect. The Mass should be the centre of our lives". The messages lament the fact that, "You do not celebrate the Eucharist as you should."

On occasions these weapons of salvation are brought together into a single message, "Pray! Pray! It is necessary to believe firmly, to go to confession regularly, and, likewise, to receive Holy Communion. It is the only salvation".

Peace

One of the other underlying and persistent themes is that of Peace: individuals seeking peace in their own hearts and then transmitting that peace to others, in what should be a cumulative effect that embraces families, communities and eventually nations. "I am your Mother, and the Queen of Peace".

This desire for peace within the messages manifested itself in an extraordinary way in the very early days, when it was reported that the parish priest, Father Jozo, wishing to publicly consolidate his own conviction and conversion, called together the parishioners to explain his position. Having done that, he then challenged them to take up his example, defying anyone to leave the church until they had demonstrated forgiveness. Then, as described by Wayne Weible in *'The Final Harvest'*: "He then folded his arms and waited. There was an uneasy shifting, and a low, continuous murmur. Finally, a burly villager stood up, red faced and nervous. He walked over to another man with whom he had feuded for years, and stuck out his hand. The man stood up, but instead of taking his hand embraced him, a rare act between Croatian men so hardened by daily toil and years of oppression. In seconds the church was a happy bedlam as mass forgiveness began the conversion process for Medjugorje."

The different religions

Whilst the emphasis of the messages is on the 'five weapons of salvation', they occasionally address specific issues. One notable one, in January 1985, seemed to have clearly affirmed Church teaching and positively encouraged ecumenism and interfaith considerations. It reportedly came about by the questioning of a Catholic priest who had difficulty in understanding why a gypsy child, not only not of the faith, but also one of the despised ethnic enemy, could be healed through the intercession of the Mother of God. The response was reported as: "Tell this priest, tell everyone, that it is you who are divided on earth. The Muslims and the Orthodox, for the same reason as Catholics, are equal before my Son and me. You are all my children. Certainly all religions are not equal, but all men are equal before God, as St Paul says. It does not suffice to belong to the Catholic Church to be saved, but it is necessary to respect the commandments of God in following one's conscience. Those who are not Catholics, are no less creatures made in the image of God, and destined to rejoin someday the House of the Father. Salvation is available to everyone without exception. Only those who refuse God deliberately are condemned".

The reference to St Paul is from his letter to the Romans, "... as one man's trespass led to condemnation for all men, so one man's act of righteousness leads to acquittal and life for all men" (*Rm* 5:18). The Church carries this through by stating, "Those who, through no fault of their own do not know the Gospel of Christ or his Church, but who nevertheless seek God with a sincere heart, and, moved by grace, try in their actions to do His will as they know it through the dictates of their conscience

- those too may achieve eternal salvation" (*Lumen Gentium* 16). Specifically with regard to Muslims, "The plan of salvation also includes those who acknowledge the Creator, in the first place amongst whom are the Muslims; these profess to hold the faith of Abraham, and together with us they adore the one, merciful God, mankind's judge on the last day" (*CCC 841*).

Compassion

In rather more prosaic matters, the human touch is also reflected in the messages. Care and compassion is shown, whether it be for individuals, groups or indeed the whole world, "I invite you to do works of mercy with love and out of love for me and your brothers and sisters"; "I offer your sacrifices and prayers to God for the salvation of the world". There is the reminder from the ever-constant salutation "Dear children" that precede the messages, that she is our mother too. The seers have also reported her consideration for them: she has never insisted that they follow any course of consecrated life, and with some regret she realistically foretold that their lives would never be easy.

Prayer conquers evil

There are no punches pulled in the head-on use in the messages of the word 'Satan' and all that that he portrays, and with this word disdain, yet not underestimation, of him and his evil designs, is clearly portrayed. "Satan is working even more violently to take the joy away from each of you. Through prayer you can totally disarm him and ensure your happiness", "Satan is so strong. With all his power he wants to thwart the plans I have undertaken with you. You must only pray", but in amongst these warnings, reassurance as well, "Satan's plan has failed".

The Ten Secrets

The visionaries have stated that the urgency and the reality of the messages have been emphasised by ten secrets entrusted to them by Our Lady. These secrets are said to reveal the consequences of humanity failing to correct itself. To date three of the visionaries have testified that they have received all ten secrets, the other three have been given nine so far. The visionaries have also affirmed that when the apparitions cease at Medjugorje, they will also cease at other sites round the world, and when this happens the secrets will begin to be revealed.

What little is known of the secrets were given in a letter written in 1982 to the Pope and the Bishop of Mostar by Father Tomislav Vlasic, the local pastor at the time, as part of the initial report on the happenings at Medjugorje (as quoted below). In summary they declare that, "This time is a period of grace and conversion", but also a "chastisement for the sins of the world", and, "For that reason the Blessed Virgin calls for urgent conversion and reconciliation". Initially three warnings will be given to the world. After these three, a visible sign will be made at the place of the apparitions at Medjugorje as indication of serious intent and authenticity, and as a call back to faith. Mirjana has been chosen to testify these secrets, and ten days before she will notify Father Petar Ljubicic, who will pray and fast for seven days prior to announcing them to the world. Mirjana has been reported as saying, "...the first secret will break the power of satan, and that is why he is so aggressive now".

After the first warnings it is said that the others will follow, "within a rather brief period of time, so that people will have time for conversion". The evil reported of the seventh secret has already been mitigated through prayer and fasting; as for the ninth and tenth secrets they, "are grave matters", but of which, "the chastisement can be mitigated by prayers and penance".

The seeming level of this predetermination is not characteristic of past Marian apparitions, and whilst God has revealed of the 'end times' "...of that day and hour no one knows, not even the angels of heaven, but the Father only" (*Mt* 24:36,37), there would appear to be indication that there could be time, albeit brief, for repentance and conversion, and maybe a chance for the human race to petition God for reprieve as it did at Nineveh. It may also be appropriate here to reflect again on Cardinal Ratzinger's words on private revelations, "In every age the Church has received the charism of prophecy, which must be scrutinised but not scorned. On this point it should be kept in mind that prophecy in the biblical sense does not mean to predict the future but to explain the will of God for the present, and therefore show the right path to take for the future ...".

Our Lady's place regarding Jesus

There are many people who have reservations about 'Marian apparitions' since they are all just about Mary - a Mary who eclipses her Son, and in fact begs competition for our favours and attention. However some would argue that when looking at the Medjugorje messages a consistent theme of reverence and respect for Jesus may be detected, whether it be the habitual greeting "Praised be Jesus", or recurring reference such as, "My Son Jesus Christ wishes to bestow special graces on you through me", "Pray and ask for the grace of God, I will pray that He gives them to you", and always, "My heart rejoices because of Jesus". Further, when reading the messages, a loving and subordinate relationship with God emerges.

There are many who believe that the Medjugorje messages also portray a relationship that is wholly Trinitarian in character, "... pray for an outpouring of the Holy Spirit", "I will pray to my Son, Jesus ...", "You do not know how many graces God is bestowing upon you these days when the Holy Spirit is working in a special way". "Open your hearts to the Holy Spirit. Especially during these days the Holy Spirit is working through you. Open your hearts and surrender your life to Jesus so that he works through your hearts".

VIEWPOINTS

Generally

Events such as those reported from Medjugorje seem to generate disquiet, for somehow they encompass and test the whole spectrum of faith and credibility, from the strength of our beliefs, all the way through to the weaknesses of our disbeliefs. The fact that the Church does not require any individual to accept the officially approved apparitions of the post-apostolic era, such as Fatima or Lourdes, 'with the certitude of divine faith' must emphasise this fact. But the very fact that the Church, as the Body of Christ, *does* accept and approve certain apparition events must give credence and substance to their reality. In this particular context Karl Rahner asserts, "Therefore the essence of all private revelations after Christ must be such as to fit into eschatalogical salvific reality". He goes on, "Anyone who absolutely rejects the possibility of special revelations offends against faith; and anyone who denies that they occur even since the apostolic age, offends against a doctrine which is theologically certain".

Medjugorje

The Church with regard to Medjugorje has made its position clear in 1991, by way of the Zadar Declaration 'on the basis of the investigation so far it cannot be affirmed that one is dealing with supernatural apparitions and revelations.' Cardinal Ratzinger, speaking in November 1984 about Medjugorje in the Italian monthly review, *Jesus*, was reported as saying, "Revelation was completed by Jesus Christ, who is Himself our revelation. Nevertheless, we cannot deny that God could speak to our own age, even through humble or simple people and through extraordinary signs, to expose the shortcomings of a culture imbued with rationalism, as is the case with ours".

Of the great contemporary theologians, the late Cardinal-designate Father Hans Urs von Balthasar was quite specific about relating to events at Medjugorje. His verdict, published in an interview by the UK's *Catholic Herald* in November 1985, was that, "its theology rings true. I am convinced of its truth. And everything about Medjugorje is true in a Catholic sense. What is happening there is so evident, so convincing".

In 1988, Cardinal Christoph Schonborn, the Archbishop of Vienna, in a personal testament that he gave at Lourdes, also spoke about Medjugorje, "Personally, I have not been to Medjugorje, but in a certain way I have been there many times through the people I have met and the people I know. And in their lives I am seeing good fruit. I would be lying if I said this fruit did not exist. This fruit is concrete and visible and I can see in our diocese and in many other places, graces of conversion, graces of a supernatural life of faith, graces of joy, graces of vocations, of healings, of people returning to the Sacraments - to confession. All this is not misleading. Therefore, as far as I am concerned as a Bishop, I can only see the fruit. If we had to judge the tree by its fruit, like Jesus, I must say that the tree is fruitful!"

The three views above pre-date Zadar. There have been individual views expressed since then which are similarly positive. Msgr Gilbert Aubry, Bishop of St Denis (Reunion Island), writes in the Preface to Sister Emmanuel's book *'Medjugorje, the 90s'*, "... in the middle of winter I went secretly to Medjugorje with, in my heart, the full weight of twenty years as a bishop. I went to ask forgiveness for my failings and to give thanks. I climbed up Mt Krizevac, sometimes on my knees, tears running down my face. In my chest there beat a heart of such gentleness and humility that it didn't feel like me ... My Lord, and my God, it isn't me anymore! I left Medjugorje at fifty three years of age with all the strength of a new heart and a new spirit, ready for the mission that both fills me with burning passion, and carries me as well: all is joy and hope, thirst for justice and peace, with Mary. Today I bear witness".

In July 2000, Msgr Leonard André-Mutien of Namour, Belgium, in an echo of Pope Urban's statement on belief in apparitions, acknowledged that there were risks in believing what was going on at Medjugorje. He describes them as contradictory risks - the one of being deceived, and the other of bypassing a gift of grace. He is reported as preferring to take the risk of being open and receiving the grace of belief.

There are certainly an unknown number of people who have reservations or disbelief about Medjugorje, in degrees ranging from healthy scepticism to sheer disbelief. There are people who think that the happenings at Medjugorje are pure hoax, being manipulated by the Franciscans for nationalistic and political reasons and connived over by the seers and others for personal and commercial gain.

Equally, there is an unknown number who, observing the proliferation of material in favour of Medjugorje in the form of books, devotional publications, web sites, active organisations and prayer groups, think that on this balance of evidence - and disregarding any claims to supernatural input - there is something positive and good emanating from this place - something that people wish to read and think about.

The Holy Father, by virtue of his position as the Vicar of Christ prudently and prayerfully observes the Church's current position over Medjugorje.

The growing numbers of pilgrims

What is also measurable, but in more specific terms alongside those world-wide organisations and prayer groups emanating from Medjugorje, is one of the other visible effects, and that is the twenty million or so pilgrims who have been to

Medjugorje. Accurate record keeping of pilgrim visitors only started in 1985, and then only in the form of consecrated hosts distributed - which in itself can only indicate a shortfall of the actual totals in Medjugorje. In 1985 close to half a million hosts were distributed, this steadily climbed to a peak of 1.4 million in 1990, took a dip during the war to a quarter of a million in 1992, and since the end of the war has generally shown a steady year on year increase to 1.2 million in 2001. Similarly, the figures for concelebrating priests were only started in 1986, when 7,438 are recorded as visiting. The average over recent years is about 23,000 a year, giving an overall figure of 300,000 who have visited since 1986.

Increasing interest - what next?

Whilst this is only a tiny proportion of the total members of the Church, it is still a substantial body who have had to make special effort and incur the expense to make this journey; the Church world-wide is also plainly represented, as are the clergy from senior to junior. Add to this the world-wide prayer groups and organisations, there would appear to be a cumulative groundswell of the Medjugorje phenomenon beginning to display and generate a desire by the people - possibly in a faint echo of *sensus fidelium* - for the Church to approve the reported apparitions when the time of further declarations over Medjugorje comes. In Newman's words, when he was propounding his views on *sensus fidelium*, "We do unfeignedly believe ... that their

Lordships [ie the bishops] really desire to know the opinion of the laity on subjects in which the laity are especially concerned ... it is at least natural [for the Church] to anticipate such an act of kind feeling and sympathy in great practical questions" (*The Rambler*, May 1859). St Augustine certainly acknowledged the role of the Faithful in expressing and desiring approval in matters of common consensus, "It seems that I have believed nothing but the firm opinion and the exceedingly widespread report of populations and nations".

In addressing us as "My dear friends", the Evangelist John exhorts us to "... test the spirits to see whether they are from God, for many false prophets are at large in the world" (1 *Jn* 4:1). If these spirits do indeed come from God they will be known by their fruits, as attested by Matthew in his Gospel, "A sound tree cannot bear bad fruit" (*Mt* 7:18). They will also be tested by their relationship with God, "Whoever says 'I know him' without keeping his commandments is a liar" (1 *Jn* 2:3,4); but especially in what they say of Christ, "... any spirit which acknowledges Jesus Christ, come in human nature, is from God" (1 *Jn* 4:2).

To go, or not to go?

In terms of status Medjugorje is simply a parish with its parish church of St James the Apostle. In those terms there are no reasons not to visit. In reality, it is of course a parish church very much out of the ordinary, because it is geared - efficiently, yet modestly, geared - for a huge influx of visitors, coping with numbers far in excess of that for any normal parish. The reasons for this influx will now be well known to the reader. The question now may be: to go or not to go?

The legitimacy and question of conscience of going to Medjugorje should not pose a problem. In personally weighing up this decision it may be helpful to look again at the ruling given in the Zadar Declaration, which is still the Church's current position:

• "On the basis of the investigations so far it cannot be affirmed that one is dealing with supernatural apparitions and revelations". In practical terms this leaves the case open for further investigation, as emphasised by the Director of the Vatican Press Office in June 1996 (*Bulletin No 233*), "One must still repeatedly emphasise the indispensable necessity of continuing the search and the reflection, besides the prayer, in the face of any presumed supernatural phenomenon, as long as there be no definitive pronouncement". This was subsequently reinforced by Archbishop Bertone from CDF when he stated in 1998 "... it would now pertain to the members of the Episcopal Conference of Bosnia-Herzegovina to perhaps reopen the examination of this case, and to make any new pronouncements that might be called for." (Full text at Appendix).

• "The numerous gatherings of the faithful ... require the attention and pastoral care ... of the bishops [so that] a healthy devotion to the Blessed Virgin Mary may be promoted in accordance with the teachings of the Church". Private pilgrimages, accompanied by suitable pastoral support, are therefore permitted under the condition that they are not, to quote Archbishop Bertone again, "understood as recognition of the events which are still happening and which still demand to be examined by the Church". In a clarification by the Vatican Press Office (August 1996) that previous statements by Archbishop Bertone could be misinterpreted as a complete ban on any form of pilgrimage to Medjugorje, the Vatican spokesman, Dr Joaquin Navarro-Valls, concluded by saying, "I was worried that what Archbishop Bertone said could be interpreted in too restricted a way. Has the Church or the Vatican said "no" to Medjugorje? No."

There is therefore no bar whatsoever to the laity organising themselves as individuals or into pilgrim groups to make the journey to Medjugorje, accompanied by their parish, or any other priest, to tend to their pastoral needs. General worship and the veneration of Our Lady at Medjugorje is strictly within limits of Church teaching, practice and accepted liturgy, and is kept that way under the watchful eyes of the Franciscans.

As far as the view of the local Bishop, the Bishop of Mostar, it is clear, as stated by Archbishop Bertone of the CDF, that his position is to be, "considered the expression of the personal conviction of [his] which he has the right to express as Ordinary of the place, but which is, and remains, his personal opinion".

The practicalities

The practicalities of going are not difficult either: the Catholic press regularly advertises travel companies that specialise in arranging pilgrimages to Medjugorje either as groups, or individuals. Travel by these companies is in modern aircraft and coaches. Most of these tour companies provide couriers that accompany groups and co-ordinate, suggest or arrange pilgrim events in and around Medjugorje, which the casual visitor on restricted time and information may miss. From my own very limited experience, this was all conducted within a reverent and prayerful atmosphere. Accommodation in the pensions was simple but perfectly adequate, and actually suited one's mood of pilgrimage; it was also in a very welcoming, family atmosphere. There is of course nothing to stop the more adventurous (or penurious!) pilgrim seeking other routes and methods of getting there.

At the time of writing prices locally were very reasonable; a certain mental dexterity was required as any form of currency seemed acceptable, and rates of exchange seemed flexible! Movement round the further reaches of the town is generally best made in one of the many taxis, offering friendly service and fixed price journeys. Warm clothing and waterproofs in winter is recommended, and good walking shoes/boots or substantial trainers at any time of the year should aid the ascent of Krizevac and Apparition Hill.

Personal Pilgrimage and Fruits

In common with many pilgrims over the years, I suspect I went to Medjugorje with a strange and contradictory blend of curiosity, faith, hope, and a desire to be open-minded. Always lurking in the background, though, was that grating vein of scepticism that taunts most believers, and curiosity as to why this humble rural village should be the focus of such huge attention. Faith in the numbers: that those twenty million people who had seen fit, or been in some way called to make this eccentric pilgrimage, did so for reasons other than just plain curiosity. Hope, that the experience would help to strengthen my faith. Open-mindedness that my newly rediscovered and regenerated faith would sustain a non-judgemental approach until the evidence, one way or another, had been revealed and could be evaluated. As for that nagging scepticism, it would have to be actively confronted on a daily basis and weighed against the evidence, rather than conveniently buried and ignored.

First impressions

Arriving in Medjugorje in the early hours gave little scope for first impressions, apart from the very hospitable welcome and meal from our hosts at our pension. On wandering into town after breakfast, my diary records, "... immediate thoughts were that of a small frontier town - still with an atmosphere of charm and naïvety, still with an unpolished, unsophisticated and unfinished air, still a place where you felt safe and without the need to cling close to your bag". Despite the hundreds of pilgrims who visit and stay every day, there are no swanky hotels, no air conditioned shopping malls or tacky games arcades.

Dominating the town is the clean, simple and modern lines of the parish church of Saint James with its elegant twin clock towers. Surrounding the church are large plaza areas to accommodate the many thousands of over-spill pilgrims during popular devotional days and periods. Down one side are rows of custom-built confessionals, indicative of one of the church's main purposes and activities. Quietly gracing the far end of the main approach plaza is a humble, serene and demure statue of Our Lady, hand outstretched in a gentle, never ending invitation.

One is also very quickly struck by the quiet but purposeful and busy air about the place. The faces of many nations are present - faces that give powerful witness to the universality of the Catholic Church and the wide spread of the Medjugorje phenomena. In the town, activity naturally centres around the church. There is a substantial ebb and flow of pilgrims joining and leaving the back-to-back Masses in many languages. The evening devotion of the local community is inspiring and outstanding, with a daily three hour worship period of all Mysteries of the Rosary, Mass and prayer. At twenty to seven the recital of the Rosary comes to a halt during the period when the apparitions are reported as occurring, and there follows, "a lovely reflective but highly charged period during which a violin softly played lending a serenity to those hundreds of the faithful totally absorbed with their inner contemplation" (*my diary*).

There are not only the faces of the many nations present, but also all ages. Medjugorje, however, does mean a special place for the youth of the world, because it is here that the young people have been gathering annually to celebrate their Faith and their Church. It was against the foreboding background of war clouds in 1989, that on the eighth anniversary there was a gathering of thousands of young people in Medjugorje for the first organised youth festival to mark the Year of Youth. It was from a subsequent, similar gathering in Medjugorje in 1990 that Youth 2000 emerged, which continues to thrive and grow in many countries round the world (cf. CTS booklet *Youth 2000*) - another of the visible fruits of Medjugorje, and the fast ripening fruit for harvest in future years.

Activities in Medjugorje

Of the other activities in the immediate environs of the town are a constant series of talks and seminars during the day, held in a large new lecture hall close to the church with a very striking mural of Our Lady. The talks are given by the visionaries themselves, local priests or other resident or visiting speakers. My

diary records, "went to a talk by Ivan, one of the
visionaries. I was impressed by the dignity with which
he spoke, and the way he patiently and courteously
answered questions from pilgrims that must have been
asked thousands of times before, and that he was not
mobbed afterwards."

There is a Blessed Sacrament chapel close to the
church which allows periods of Adoration and quiet
prayer away from the hurly burly of activities in the
main church. In the Communities and houses in the
town, other devotions, talks and seminars are under
way, such as those run by Sister Emmanuel of the
Beatitudes, who "gave a wide-ranging and thought-
provoking talk, with her love of Jesus and Our Lady
shining out. She described Medjugorje as 'a time of
great mercy as never before'".

On the wider outskirts of the compact town,
interspersed with small vineyards and other cultivated
fields, are other visible and moving fruits of
Medjugorje, amongst which are the separate boys' and
girls' *Cenacolo* Communities, the Oasis of Peace
Community, and Mothers' Village - an orphanage and
home for single mothers and their children. I say visible
fruits, because whatever one's personal opinion may be
about the reported happenings at Medjugorje, the
inspiring and tangible endeavours of every day at
Medjugorje remain impressive.

The *Cenacolo*

To me one of the most moving experiences was our visit to the male *Cenacolo*, described as "a Christian association that welcomes lost, unsatisfied, and desperate young people who want to find themselves again, to find joy in life, and to find meaning for their lives". The movement was founded in 1983 by an Italian nun, Sister Elvira, who wanted to give her life to God by helping drug addicts and young people who despaired of the world. Currently there are 27 *Cenacolos* round the world. It is an extraordinary community of young people who run it by themselves for themselves; there is no outside assistance of any sort (except in medical emergency); and it literally means this, from the management of the institution, to the daily chores of cooking and cleaning, to the major construction work of designing and building their accommodation. They live frugal, hard working, self regulated lives of work and prayer, and of love, through ceaselessly looking after and caring for each other.

In one major example of what the community stands for, the two young men giving their testimony ruefully described the realisation that, when during the construction of one of their accommodation blocks, two joining walls were going to be seriously out of line: they had no option but to demolish and start again. "But," one of them said, "it is not about building houses that we are here, it is about rebuilding lives". My diary goes on, "also crucial to this

process was each individual being told and confronted with
the truth about himself." Their testimony was given in the
most exquisite modern chapel, where every item, including
the pews, stained glass windows and large striking and
vibrant icon painting of the Resurrection, was designed,
manufactured and built by themselves.

Krizevac - the Hill of the Cross

If it is the church of St James that dominates the immediate
town, it is the Hill of the Cross (*Krizevac*) with its plain,
stark concrete cross that dominates the local area. It is a
steep, rugged, rocky hill with a constant stream of pilgrims,
which, singly or in small informal groups or larger tour
parties - some painfully barefooted - wend their way
upwards, following the exquisitely sculpted bronze reliefs
of the Stations of the Cross. On ascending, one hears the
Stations being venerated in every language of the world.

I followed the Stations twice when I was in
Medjugorje. The most memorable and meaningful was
on my own, undertaken at five in the morning - still
dark - working my way up by torchlight until the dawn
started breaking, then, "Most sublime moment when
praying at the Twelfth, the Crucifixion, I lifted my head
up to the sculpture of the tortured, crucified Christ at
the very moment that the rising sun hit it full-on,
bathing this scene of agony and sacrifice in a strong,
golden, liberating light".

This was also quite an unusual set of Stations, with the additional fifteenth, the Resurrection, near the top by the Cross of Krizevac. It was the place where Father Slavko Barbaric, the revered Franciscan of Medjugorje, and Spiritual Director to the 'visionaries', died suddenly of a heart attack on 24th November 2001, having just led a group of pilgrims along the Stations. The monthly message the next day was reported as giving assurance that, "... your brother Slavko has been born into Heaven and intercedes for you".

Work of the visionaries

There are also many activities in and around the town that are led by the visionaries. On our first full night, Ivan reported that he was due to receive a special apparition during a gathering of his prayer group at ten o'clock. He had made this known and had invited pilgrims to be present. "The gathering was hushed and muted, and I felt privileged to share with this ordinary young man, at the very least, his own moments of reverence and prayer. Others of our group felt it no more than 'standing on a wet hillside at night with a whole lot of other people doing exactly the same'". This of course was one of the first 'scepticism tests' of the visit.

However, the answer to my scepticism came from a quite unexpected direction. On the fifth day our group was invited to the house of Vicka, one of the visionaries,

to hear her talk about Our Lady. As we approached down
the narrow village road I could see quite a sizeable crowd
gathered around the raised patio of one of the terraced
houses. My heart sank at the prospect of an international
bun fight just to catch a glimpse of Vicka - Mr Scepticism
was nagging at me again. In the event, seeing her was not
a problem, as when she appeared she stood on some
elevated steps. Hearing was not a problem, either, as her
words were amplified by loudspeaker. It was her second
'session' of the day. In normal circumstances she would
not turn heads in a crowd - a slim, sallow complexioned,
37 year old woman with high cheek bones, dark hair and
dark eyes. She starts to speak. Her face is immediately lit
by a continuous and generous smile.

She speaks passionately and eloquently in Italian
(translated into English). She of course speaks about Our
Lady and what she requires of us. She also acknowledges,
in a modest and grateful way, the waves and blown kisses
of the pilgrims energetically trying to catch her attention.
She has been doing all this for twenty years, during which
some of the time she has suffered painful illness. In the
early days under communism this behaviour brought
strife to her family and village; and nowadays that
message has completely forfeited her private life

And then for me an extraordinary episode. Vicka, we are
told, usually concludes with a short period of meditation
and prayer, but on this occasion, she slipped into a deep,

concentrated and sustained trance-like state; her face was serene and peaceful. She stood there for half an hour, totally absorbed, completely still, oblivious to the outside world.

After this she could easily have disappeared back into the house, but, probably as many hundreds of times before, she patiently talked to every single pilgrim that approached her.

Whilst not as steep, Apparition Hill, has the same rugged and unforgiving terrain as the Hill of the Cross. But it also has a tranquil, peaceful air, as it is a place where the apparitions are reported as happening. The Mysteries of the Rosary, in the same dramatic bronze reliefs as the Stations on Krizevac, wend their way round the hillside, with the faithful following their course. The place of the apparitions is marked by a huge Tyrolean Crucifix presented by the people of Bolzano, in South Tyrol. It sits in an area cleared to bare rock by the thousands of pilgrim feet, and in this small bowl those pilgrims sit or kneel, sunk in deep thought, prayer or meditation, seeking solace or giving thanks.

Beyond Medjugorje

Beyond Medjugorje pilgrims have the opportunity to wander further afield. One of the most frequent stops is at the Church of the Immaculate Conception of the Blessed Virgin Mary in nearby Tihaljina. It is to this church, that the first parish priest of the apparitions, Father Jozo, brought the now world famous statue of Our Lady, the statue that to most Medjugorje pilgrims evokes the image of Our Lady Queen of Peace.

Then on to Siroki Brijeg, one of the oldest Franciscan monasteries in Herzegovina, and the scene of a horrendous burning to death of 12 Franciscans by partisans in 1945. It was here that, "the inspirational Father Jozo Zovko gave an outstandingly humble and spiritually charged talk, handing out cards and rosaries, and commissioning us to go out and actively give witness to the Gospel message." Afterwards we were all invited to a powerful session of individual blessing conducted by Father Jozo and assisted by other priests in the spacious church.

During our six days at Medjugorje we experienced probably a lifetime of spiritual input, certainly enough to gently process in a lifetime.

Testimonies

Of course there is the 'health warning' that goes with all the foregoing. Some have gone to Medjugorje with inflated anticipation and unreal expectation. However there are many thousands of testimonies coming out of Medjugorje. Stefan Park's is one example. Stefan, a Scot, was a lapsed Catholic, and for many years his life "became endless darkness as a result of self-centred fulfilment". In desperation he started turning back to God, who, "appeared to be deaf to my prayers, before answering in dramatic fashion. The summer of 1985 saw me on holiday in Dubrovnic waiting for three days to join up with some friends. I was bored on my own, and whilst considering how to amuse myself, the words of a Sunday Times article from a couple of years back were put into my mind: 'Medjugorje - people are going there and being changed'. I caught a bus to Medjugorje that day. Apart from the vibrancy and charged atmosphere of the place, what completely penetrated my heart was the intense and visible expression of faith being shown by the local people as they worshipped - this patent and tangible sincerity in effect triggered the start of my conversion experience. And with all these things came great joy and willingness to do anything for God".

Whilst it is reported that some pilgrims assert supernatural experiences at or after returning from Medjugorje, Stefan's experience, and many like him, was effected by 'normal' visible and quite un-sensational means, through human example and inspiration. Stefan's life continued its dramatic course when on 13th October 2001, he was ordained an Augustinian priest. In his words, "God is amazing!".

APPENDIX

Text of the letter from Archbishop Tarcisio Bertone, Secretary, Congregation for the Doctrine of the Faith, to Bishop Gilbert Aubry, Bishop of Saint Denis on Reunion Island.

26th May 1998

Excellency,

In your letter of 1st January 1998, you submitted to this Dicastery several questions about the position of the Holy See and of the Bishop of Mostar in regard to the so-called 'apparitions' of Medjugorje, private pilgrimages, and the pastoral care of the faithful who go there.

In regard to this matter I think it is impossible to reply to each of the questions posed by your Excellency - The main thing I would like to point out is that the Holy See does not ordinarily take a position of its own regarding supposed supernatural phenomena as a court of first instance. As for the credibility of the 'apparitions' in question, this Dicastery respects what was decided by the Bishops of the former Yugoslavia in the Zadar Declaration of 10th April 1991: "... On the basis of the investigations so far, it cannot be affirmed that one is dealing with supernatural apparitions and revelations".

Since the division of Yugoslavia into different independent nations, it would now pertain to the members of the Episcopal Conference of Bosnia-Herzegovina to eventually reopen the examination of this case and make any new pronouncements that might be called for.

What Bishop Peric [Bishop of Mostar] said in his letter to the Secretary General of 'Famille Chretienne', declaring: "My conviction and my position is not only *'non constat de supernaturalitate'*, but likewise: *'constat de non supernaturalitate'* of the apparitions or revelations of Medjugorje", should be considered the expression of the personal conviction of the Bishop of Mostar, which he has the right to express as Ordinary of the place, but which is and remains his personal opinion.

Finally, as regards pilgrimages to Medjugorje which are conducted privately, this Congregation points out that they are permitted, on condition that they are not regarded as an authentication of events still taking place and which still call for examination by the Church.

I hope I have replied satisfactorily at least to the principal questions that you have presented to this Dicastery, and I beg Your Excellency, to accept the expression of my devoted sentiments.

✝ Tarcisio Bertone

Select Bibliography

The Holy Bible. The New Jerusalem Bible (Study Edition), Dartman Longman and Todd Ltd., London, 1994.

Catechism of the Catholic Church. Geoffrey Chapman, London, 1999.

CONGREGATION FOR THE DOCTRINE OF FAITH. *The Message of Fatima* CTS, London, 2000.

CONNELL, JAN *Queen of the Cosmos*, Paraclete Press/Centre for Peace, Ilford, Essex,1991.

FARGES, MSGR ALBERT, *Mystical Phenomena*, Burns, Oates and Washbourne Ltd., London, 1926.

FOLEY, DONAL ANTHONY. *Apparitions of Mary - Their Meaning in History*. CTS London 2000.

GRAEF, HILDA. *Mary, a History of Doctrine and Devotion*. Sheed & Ward, London & New York, 1965.

JONES, E MICHAEL. *The Medjugorje Deception*. Fidelity Press, Indiana, 1998.

KONDOR, FR LOUIS SVD (ed). *Fatima in Lucia's Own Words*. Secretariado dos Pastorhinos, Fatima, Portugal 1998.

KRALJEVIC, SVETOZAR OFM. *The Apparitions of Our Lady at Medjugorje*. Information Centre MIR Medjugorje 1999.

NUIC, DR VICTOR. *Medjugorje, Pilgrim's Monograph.* Turistica naklada d.o.o. Zagreb 2000.

O'CARROLL, MICHAEL CSSp, *Medjugorje, Facts, Documents, Theology.* Veritas Publications, Dublin, 1989.

SISTERS OF ST JOSEPH OF PHILADELPHIA. *Encyclopedic Dictionary of Religion.* Corpus Publications, Washington, 1979.

TINDAL-ROBERTSON, TIMOTHY. *Fatima in the Third Millennium.* CTS, London 2002.

VARIOUS, *I am Your Mother. I come to be with you.* The Association of the Pilgrim Virgin, Powys, 2001.

WEIBLE, WAYNE *The Final Harvest.* Paraclete Press, Massachusetts, 1999.

ZORZA, PIETRO *Medjugorje, Dear Children, Thank You.* Centro Grafico Lenese, Italy, 1996 (Not for sale - distributed free).

Selected websites

www.newadvent.org (Catholic Encyclopedia)
www.medjugorje.hr 'official' Medjugorje website
www.medjugorje.org.uk details for England and Wales